# The Law of
# ATTRACTION:
## Universal Power of Spirit

### Jeremy Lopez

**THE LAW OF ATTRACTION: Universal Power of Spirit**
By Dr. Jeremy Lopez
Copyright © 2014 by Jeremy Lopez

Printed and bound in the United States of America.

Published by Identity Network
P.O. Box 383213
Birmingham, AL 35238
www.identitynetwork.net
United States of America
The author can be contacted at customerservice@identitynetwork.net


Book design by
Treasure Image & Publishing
TreasureImagePublishing.com
248.403.8046

# James L. Lopez

### 1942-2014

*Dedicated to the greatest man I have ever known in my life, James Lopez. He was more than a dad and a friend; he was my hero. Until I see you again in Heaven. I love you always and forever!*

*Your son, Jeremy*

# TABLE OF CONTENTS

*The Law of Attraction*

# DEDICATION

I dedicate this book to God. Within you and through you I can accomplish anything. You are my life and strength. Thank you for showing me what grace, mercy and love is all about. May your kingdom come and your will be done on earth as it is in Heaven. Like Isaiah once said, "Here I am, send me." Use me to display your love in the earth until every nation awakens to Your love and peace.

This book is also dedicated to my parents, Pastors Jim and Jeannie Lopez. You both have been the best example of God's love I have ever known. You have been my inspiration and anchor through the good and the bad. May the glory of God continue to shine upon you both with grace, mercy and peace all the days of your life. You both awakened to your divine destiny and fulfilled it before the Lord. I love you both very much.

# Endorsements

*"You are put on this earth with incredible potential and a divine destiny. This powerful, practical man shows you how to tap into powers you didn't even know you had."*

**Brian Tracy - Author, The Power of Self-Confidence**

*"I have been privileged to have known Jeremy Lopez for many years as well as sharing the platform with him at a number of conferences. Through this time I have found him as a man of integrity, commitment, wisdom and one of the most networked people I have met. Jeremy is an entrepreneur and a leader of leaders. He has amazing insights into leadership competencies and values. He has a passion to ignite this latent potential within individuals and organizations and provide ongoing development and coaching to bring about competitive advantage and success. I would recommend him as a speaker, coach, mentor and consultant."*

**Chris Gaborit - Learning Leader, Training & Outsourcing Expert, Entrepreneur, Network Orchestrator**

*"Jeremy Lopez is a real gift. He is authentic, passionate, and has an amazing love for God, people, and life. As Founder of the Identity Network, he has been able to deliver relevant connectivity, teaching, and resources across the world. He hears the voice of God and helps others to hear God's voice for their own lives. He is an engaging speaker, and makes an impact in every community he serves. I highly recommend him."*

**Robert Ricciardelli - Talk Show Host, Social Evangelist, Thought Leader, Life/Business Coach, Growth Catalyst, Writer, Speaker**

*"Never surrender your hopes and dreams to the fateful limitations others have placed on their own lives. The vision of your true destiny does not reside within the blinkered outlook of the naysayers and the doom prophets. Judge not by their words, but accept advice based on the evidence of actual results. Do not be surprised should you find a complete absence of anything mystical or miraculous in the manifested reality of those who are so eager to advise you. Friends and family who suffer the lack of abundance, joy, love, fulfillment and prosperity in their own lives really have no business imposing their self-limiting beliefs on your reality experience."*

**Anthon St. Maarten**

# THE LAW OF ATTRACTION

A search on Google for "The Law of Attraction" will get you about 90,100,000 results! People have written about this subject from a lot of different perspectives. Many of the people that have written about it are what many of you might classify as "Spiritualist," but in actuality, the Bible, and specifically Jesus, has much to say about the Law of Attraction. Of course, you won't find it called that in the Bible, but the idea is clearly presented. So in this book, I want to help you to understand and be able to apply to your life the Law of Attraction from a God perspective.

Simply stated, the Law of Attraction is this: *What you focus your thoughts and attention on will be manifested in your life.* There are also two axioms to this law, which are *Like attracts like* and *Thoughts become things.* We will examine these statements and how to apply them in some detail, but first there are some concepts and terminology that we need to understand, because I will refer to them throughout this book. Some of the terminology that I use is shared by New Thought, spiritualists and other people who are not necessarily Christian. So to those of my readers who are Christian, I encourage you to have an open mind. Words are just words, they don't belong to any specific religion or system, if they are useful to explain an idea, I will use them. Words are, however, powerful, and there is power in the belief or emotions behind our words. God spoke the Universe into existence with just two words! (In the Hebrew, *yehi 'or*, "Let there be light.")

# Definitions

**Spirit:** God is spirit, as we know and understand from the Bible. We are the only other things in creation that we know of that have a spirit: eternal, unborn and undying. A human being is a spirit having a human experience. Our spirits were marked off in God before time began. See my book, *Abandoned to Divine Destiny* for more about this concept. Now all spirit is connected, is one, and our true self, our spirit is eternal, unlimited, existing <u>now</u> in eternity.

**Human Being:** A human being has three parts, the eternal spirit, the soul, and the body. The soul and the body were designed to serve the spirit as its medium for experiencing life on Earth. The soul is our mind, will and emotions, and is the conduit, the connection between the spiritual and the physical. The body is the vessel or physical instrument by which we experience the world around us.

**Now Moment:** Our spirit lives in eternity, but our human experience is lived out in time. The *Now Moment* is where time and eternity intersect in our awareness. Those who understand who they are in Christ remember their past and plan for the future, but they dwell in the Now. They do not fragment themselves and live in the past or the future, which is where those who are ruled by the body and the soul dwell.

**Empowerment:** Thoughts are energy, and what we focus our thoughts and attention on become empowered.

**Frequency:** All energy travels in frequency waves, from the lowest (longest) wavelength of radio waves to the highest (shortest) wavelengths of gamma rays. Albert Einstein showed us that matter is simply condensed energy with his famous formula, $E=MC^2$, and science has determined that every particle of matter vibrates at certain frequencies. Our thoughts and emotions are forms of energy, so naturally they have different frequencies. Bad or sad thoughts or emotions have lower frequencies and happy or joyful thoughts and emotions have higher frequencies.

**The Mind of Christ (or God):** also referred to as Christ Consciousness. When our spirit is awakened and we align ourselves with the will of God, and allow God's Spirit to dwell in us, then we begin to live in *Christ Consciousness.* Our spirit and God's Spirit act in unison, and our consciousness is expanded beyond our natural, human capacity. Paul tells us in I Corinthians 2:16, "For who hath known the mind of the LORD that he may instruct him? But we have the mind of Christ."

# Foundational Principles

We see the Law of Attraction at work in the life of Jesus from the very beginning. The Bible makes it clear from beginning to end that Jesus was the Son of God, the King of kings, Lord of lords, High Priest that sits at the right hand of God the Father. We read in the Gospels the beautiful story of how the Holy Spirit impregnated Mary, and she brought forth this amazing begotten Son called Jesus. Even on the day that he was born, Jesus knew that he was a king. The Christ consciousness within him knew that he was the I AM, the Son of the Living God. And in that Now Moment, kings from afar, the Magi, began to come, bringing precious gifts fit for a king - gold, frankincense and myrrh. Why did they do this? It was because he already owned those titles. He already died before the foundation of the world. Christ already knew who he was. His identity, consciousness and his whole being knew that he was the King of kings and Lord of lords; the Prince of Peace, Jehovah Jirah, our provider; God made flesh, dwelling among us. And so these kings came from afar, bringing precious gifts in fulfillment of that which he was. Like attracts like. The things that were appropriate to his identity were drawn to him. It worked for Jesus and it will work for us.

You won't find the Law of Attraction called by that name in the Bible, but it is a kingdom principle or law that can be found throughout the Bible, and especially in the teachings of Jesus. Now, thousands of years later we are beginning to make this law clear. You can observe it in people's lives, and there is proof of these principles. Things are manifested according to what we are thinking.

God has set the Law of Attraction at work in the Universe. You can be religious and call it "Creation" if you like, but we shouldn't be afraid of the word. God created the Universe: by the span of his hands he set the heavens—the stars and planets, galaxies and nebulae, etc. for his glory (Isaiah 40:12). The Heavens declare the Glory of God. You can call it "Creation" but it's better to understand the truth, and call it by word we use in our modern understanding, the "Universe."

God created this awesome, amazing universe for us; and everything in the universe is drawn to us according to what we think. Where does God draw these things from? He draws them from that which he has already created. And if it hasn't already been created, he will begin to birth it forth into existence by you thinking it. He brings forth things that have already been created, or things that have not yet been created, but either way you will begin to have the things that you think about, so you have to be careful about what you set your attention on.

Your mind is powerful, and what you set your thoughts, focus and attention on is empowered. Now we are not bound by the laws of the Old Testament, but are "under a better covenant, which was established upon better promises" (Hebrews 8:6). In the Old Testament, we are commanded "Thou shalt not make thee any graven image, or any likeness of anything that is in heaven above, or that is in the earth beneath, or that is in the waters beneath the earth..." (Deuteronomy 5:8). So we may be somewhere and see a statue of a Buddha, or some Hindu god. Now according to the Old Testament, these would be

21

"graven images" and God said not to have any of these before him. But we have to understand that it's not the physical object, a thing carved out of wood or stone that causes it to be a "graven image." It's the power of the emotion, the experience or the paradigm in our mind; it's the love or hate that we have for the object that empowers it. So if we look at a statue and think, "graven image...run from it, cast it down, God doesn't want it before him," we're forgetting that we live under the New Covenant. The natural came first, and then the spirit. The physical image is the natural, but even under the Old Covenant, what God looked at was the heart. It is the heart of the matter behind a thing, which is important.

You might be in the home of a Christian, and in their backyard they have a Zen garden and a koi pond with a statue of a Buddha and other Asian décor, because they admire Asian culture and style. It's not a graven image unless they empower it to be a graven image. Unless they give it their attention and bring it to life to themselves, bowing down and worshipping it, then it's not a graven image, it's just a decoration. So it is with the Law of Attraction. God' concern is with the thought of the heart.

We have to stop being "religious." No longer can we look at things in the natural. No longer do we know men by the flesh, but by the spirit. Paul tells us in I Corinthians 15:46 "Howbeit that was not first which is spiritual, but that which is natural; and afterward that which is spiritual." Under the Old Covenant, God cared about the natural, but even then he looked at the heart, the intentions, because he made us in his image and likeness, and he knew that our minds had a mechanism to bring forth what we desire, what we love or hate or lust after.

Jesus told us that if a man looks on a woman with lust then he has already committed adultery with her in his heart. It's no longer the natural that is significant but the spiritual. So if you have empowered something to be an idol in your mind and heart, you have broken the first commandment even if you don't have any statue or physical object you worship.

In the Kingdom of God there is no longer Jew nor Greek, slave nor free, male nor female (Galatians 3:28). God looks on the heart. God has always viewed the heart, with its thoughts and desires first and foremost above all else. Now under the New Covenant this idea explodes. It's <u>all</u> about spirit: who and what you really are inside. When God sees you, he doesn't see gender any more. He doesn't see male or female - he sees divine spirit made in the image and likeness of God.

The Bible says we suffer from a lack of knowledge (Hosea 4:6). I want to bring you to the place of knowing. And when you know, you are empowered. You understand that the Scripture says that to the pure, all things are pure (Titus 1:15), to the defiled, all things become defiled. If you feel like you are in a constant state of warfare, what do you think you are going to manifest, according to the universal principle of the Law of Attraction that God established? If you look for bad things around you, you will find it. If you look for thieves under every rock, you will find them. If you think people are evil and bad, then everyone, in your perception, will be evil or bad. But if you look for the Christ within people, you will begin to find the good in them. Jesus is the light that lights <u>every</u> human in the world (John 1:9). So we have to look at people, no matter what they're going through, no matter if bad or negative things are happening to them, and begin to pull out the light of God in them. We can't automatically write them off because they are not "Christian" and just see the bad in them. We have to awaken them.

I like to understand salvation as "awakening." I like to awaken people by saying, "Did you know that there's a light inside of you? Christ wants you to be aware that he has already paid the price for you. It's a done deal! God wants to supply your needs." So we begin to educate people, and the small candle inside of them begins to glow more and more brightly, until it becomes a raging fire as they grow in their understanding that Christ died for them, lives in and through them, and all the riches of God in the heavenlies are available for them.

And so, when we are in that beautiful backyard, with the Zen garden and koi pond, with the statue of the Buddha, we can appreciate its beauty, and not be concerned that it may be a "graven image" because it is not. We don't empower it, give it our devotion or attention because that's not what we want to draw back to ourselves. To the pure, all things are pure, and we can pull the goodness of its beauty, the goodness that God created. On every day of Creation, God looked at what he had made and said, "It is good." So when we see something, we want to say, "it is good." We want to draw out its goodness. God said it is good, not me. God made humans with their different cultures, and so we can appreciate the Asian culture that inspired that beautiful Zen garden with the koi pond and statue of the Buddha. We want to draw the good in everything to ourselves, not the negative or badness that may be there as well.

We read in Proverbs 23:7, "As [a man] thinketh in his heart, so is he." Why the heart, and not just the mind? It is because the heart holds the emotion, the desire, and the power of what you are thinking with your mind. A feeling or emotion is a prophetic word in motion that is being fulfilled from what the heart really wants to say. What your heart really wants will always be expressed in your emotions. If your heart is full of love, you emotions will be joyful. If your heart is full of hate, your emotions will be anger and rage. You emotions reveal what is in your heart.

And it's not just the heart that holds our emotions. It is a scientific fact that powerful experiences, whether good or bad, are recorded in the organs of our bodies, including our skin, which is also an organ. If you have witnessed a murder, or been raped, your body, your organs will remember that trauma. If you have experienced something beautiful, wonderful, breathtakingly awesome, your organs will record those feelings too. These things are locked up in the organs of your body. That is why when you are seeking healing for your body, the desire must not come only from your mind. It has to come from your heart and your whole body as well. Every emotion throughout your whole body has to release that healing so you can flow and walk properly in the place that God has called you for your life.

Like attracts like. What you think and desire, you will begin to draw into your existence. Thoughts become things. A lot of Christians get scared of this because they think if they have a thought about getting sick that they will draw it to themselves. If something goes wrong and they come down with a disease like cancer or leukemia or Parkinson's, they think they must have drawn this to themselves. We have to remember that we live in a fallen world where some things just happen. We don't know the answers to life and everything about it. We don't torment someone who is battling a major disease or catastrophe by telling them that they have called this in on themselves, that somewhere in their life they thought this into being. We will never in this life understand all the mysteries of the Kingdom of God. And we also have to look through the eyes of God, the eyes of Love and understand that God can trump our puny thoughts, and he always acts out of love and for our good, even when the worst happens to us.

We try to understand the mysteries of God, and begin to walk in them, but we will never fully understand. Yet through it all we have faith. Faith is the substance of things hoped for, the evidence of things not seen (Hebrews 11:1). The attitude we must have is "not my will, but your will be done, God." We don't understand everything. The Law of Attraction is not a burden where we have to be hyper-vigilant about what we think, and if something goes wrong, it is our fault. What we are called to do, though, is to think about things that are holy, think about things that are pure, that are of good report (Philippians 4:8). Whose report are you going to believe? We choose to believe the report of the Lord. If you believe what you see or hear in the natural world that is what you will see happen to you. Why? Because it has become a graven image or idol within you. You have believed and empowered it to manifest as a reality in your life.

Jesus knew who he was, his identity, from the very beginning of his life on earth, and so the things that were complementary to his identity were drawn to him. The problem with us is that all too often we think the Law of Attraction is some sort of magic, like a genie who appears and says "your wish is my command" when you rub the bottle. We think it's about focusing our attention on money so we will have money, or on a big new house, or a nice car. If we think about it hard enough we will have it. The mature person understands that this does work, but are these the things that you need to complement your identity? When you know who you are, you don't have to beg or plead for the things you need. You move from focusing your thoughts on "things" and start building your life on divine peace and rest. If you don't know your identity, material things will always dominate your thoughts. When we have a foundation of identity, as Jesus did, then we will draw those things that are beneficial to us into our lives.

Having material things is not bad. Having the finer things in life is not bad. What is important is what you do with them, how you get them and how you prioritize them. If you prioritize material things, you empower them; you make them "gods." You replace God with a thing. A few years ago a friend of mine was given the opportunity to receive a beautiful new Jaguar. She was worried about whether she should take it or not, but as she prayed and thought about it, God told her, "I don't have a problem with the things you have, as long as they don't have you." God does not have a problem with things. We have a problem with things when we put them where they are not supposed to be. Our lives are like the temple of God, with an outer court, an inner court and the holy of holies.

Material things belong in the outer court of our lives. The things we have empower us to do what we need to do. We need them; and money answers all things. As long as all the money, the cars, homes, clothes, etc. are in their proper place; they don't become "gods." There is no issue; God will continue to bless you. You will continue to have the finer things in life, and God will take you farther and deeper than you ever thought possible.

The inner court is where things of more substance belong, things that bring meaning and integrity to our lives, things that deserve our attention but not our worship. Business people and casual acquaintances belong in the outer court. You should never pull them close to you. Your friends and extended family are the sort of people that belong in the inner court. But the Holy Place is reserved for the one you are in a covenant relation with, and for your children, or the friend that understands your mind and heart and will always be there for you; that knows everything about

31

you and does not judge or condemn. The relationship of Naomi and Ruth was this "holy place" kind of relationship. "Your people are my people, where you go I will go." This is the kind of relationship where it doesn't matter what you say or do, you are healthy to be in my life and God has called you to be in my life. Throughout life and death, arguments, joy and love, we will stick closer than brothers.

We need to test all things in our lives and know where they belong. We should never mix things up. People and things that belong in the outer court need to stay there. Our minds are fertile. Whatever we impregnate our minds with is what we will have more of. Whether we understand the Law of Attraction or are completely ignorant of it, whatever permeates our mind will be manifested in our lives. The Universe couldn't care less whether what we draw to ourselves is health or unhealthy. It is under the command of our loving Heavenly Father and Savior to do what he designed it to do. You will reap what you sow. If you sow a seed of money, of love, of hate, of dishonesty, of discord, that is what you will get back and more. If you haven't examined your desires; have not determined whether or not what you have set your attention on is good for you, you will find yourself attracting things that are unhealthy, because whether it is good or bad for you, you will produce more of it. You will wake up one day with a lot of "babies" that you didn't consciously ask for, but because you set your attention on them, you set the Law of Attraction in motion, and now you have a mess.

It is much easier to make a mess than it is to clean it up. You can go into a room and destroy it in seconds. You can throw stuff around, break things and create havoc that will take a long time to fix. It may take you two seconds to break a lamp, but minutes or hours to fix. You have to sweep up the broken glass, get a new bulb. Maybe you have to buy a new lampshade, or even a whole new lamp. It takes a lot longer to clean up a mess then it does to make it in the first place.

Your life is like a tree. The roots are your identity, and whatever you focus your attention on grows out of that like branches, which sprout leaves and eventually grow fruit. Just as Jesus knew his identity, you have to know your identity, who you are, and focus your attention on things that build you up. You need to make sure that the things you think about complement your identity, flow from your identity, and grow from the root system of your identity. If your foundation is solid, fixed on who you are and what you're looking for in your life, the things you need for your life will automatically spring forth from what you think and perceive and know that you are. If you think lustful thoughts, you build a faulty foundation, one that is based on non-existence, insubstantial, and it will bring forth all sorts of undesirable things: pornography, dirty magazines, X-rated movies: things that are done behind closed doors to fulfill those desires and passions. Whatever you think about grows: branches, leaves and fruit.

This is why it is so important for us to understand the Law of Attraction. What you think, you are going to produce—but do you want to produce that in your life? David was a great king, but when he was on his rooftop and saw Bathsheba bathing, he began to think about having her. He ended up committing both adultery and murder over this affair, and God had to send Nathan the prophet to straighten him out. Even though David was forgiven, the results of that sin continued to affect him and his family for the rest of his life. It is easy to make a mess, but it takes much longer to clean it up. God has to go back and deal with the issues, the low self-esteem, and the things that caused you to do those things to begin with. David began to think about that woman, and he began to act it out: thoughts became things.

Your mind is powerful, and you can deceive yourself to think that you are hearing from God, when you are just giving way to your own desires. This is a problem among Christians, and especially in prophetic circles. Many people think they are hearing from God when they are not. Your thoughts will play games with you, and you can draw in things that are unhealthy, damaging or even fatal instead of things that are life-giving and resurrecting. It doesn't matter what your beliefs are, if you think it and focus your attention on it, you will send those thoughts out into the universe. God Almighty is going to cause the universe to give you more of what you are thinking. So you can end up with a huge mess of things you did not consciously intend for your life.

We have to train ourselves to examine what we think. We are not our thoughts, we are the observers of our thoughts, and we can learn to direct them. We have complete control over what we think. Our thoughts can be tamed, controlled, or even eradicated or killed if necessary, so we can bring forth something new. You have the power to create the thoughts that you want to have, and when you do this, you begin to move on a higher frequency.

Everything in creation has a frequency level. God, the Creator of things seen and unseen made the universe. If you want to move on a higher frequency, to go "from glory to glory" as Paul puts it, you have to begin to restructure your thoughts. You are in complete control of your thoughts, or you should be, because if you aren't, then someone else is!

You might think you can just fill your mind with scriptures like "not my will but thine be done," or "He must increase but I must decrease," but it's not about just knowing the Scriptures—it's about living and becoming the word of God. What has God said about you and your life? When you are being and becoming what God has said about you, then you can fill your mind with new thoughts that are in accordance with your God-given identity. Your mind will be filled with thoughts that come from the foundation on which you are built: what you know is real for you, who and what you are. Other thoughts will come and go, but the real thoughts will always spring forth from your spirit.

If you are dysfunctional, if you are masked by materialism and a focus on inconsequential things, then you will never move on a higher frequency. You will never go from glory to glory. You will never be who you are called to be because you are being carried by the flow. You have to be stable, rooted and grounded in that which you are, your identity, what God has created you to be. When you become that, then you will begin to see the true thoughts that spring forth out of your being. Then you will have favor and blessing, and you will have the material things that are healthy and necessary for your life.

Jesus said, "I am the way, the truth and the life." He made this statement this before he had gone to the cross and died for our sins. We understand that Jesus was slain before the foundation of the earth. He knew who he was, and he understood his purpose and mission, but how could he say this before he had accomplished this mission? Even though Jesus was the Eternal Son of God, he was born under the law (Galatians 4:4). He was not only born under the Torah, the Jewish law, but the physical laws of the universe. Just like us, he lived his human experience in time. Jesus is calling those things that are not as though they were. He knows that the moment he died, he paid the sacrifice. He was the Lamb slain from before the foundation of the world, but was now manifesting that by dying on the cross, building the foundation for people to see and believe that he had become the Way, the Truth and the Life. So he didn't say, "I am becoming," he said "I AM."

We too must call those things that are not as though they are. The Law of Attraction says, "Decree a thing and it shall come to pass." God has set into the universe hope and a bright future for each of us. So we have to declare that which is going to be in the Now Moment of our reality. We do not say, "I am becoming" this thing but that "I am" this thing. Jesus said," I am the Way, the Truth and the Life" because he knew he had always been these things, from the foundation of the earth.

You say, "I'm not Jesus, I didn't die before the foundation of the earth like he did. That's not me." But understand this: You've always been spirit. Spirits can't be born nor can they die. In Jeremiah 1:5 God says to Jeremiah, "Before I formed you in the womb, I knew you." The word "knew" in the Hebrew is "yadah" which is to know with intimacy, intercourse. Before you were in your mother's womb God "yadahed" you. God got you pregnant and lowered you into the earth realm. Your destiny and your purpose were already all wrapped up in you when you came out of your mother's womb. In my book *Abandoned to Devine Destiny* I give over a hundred scriptures about how we were in God before time began. We were born with destiny and purpose already formed in us, and God awakens that destiny when we receive Christ Jesus as our Savior. He awakens us to say, "Guess what, you have a destiny, a gift and talent in you." Our lives, our minds and thoughts have to be conducive to what we truly are, our identities. If we haven't wakened up to our identity, then we will never know who we are.

Once we awaken to our identity we realize that God's DNA is in us. He has impregnated us with purpose and life. So as we begin to live our lives according to the identity and destiny that God has given us, we have to remember that our thoughts need to be lined up with our identity. When we are transparent before the Lord, and begin to understand who and what we are, why we are here, we begin to be able to think the thoughts that will get us from where we are to where we are designed to be. This will enable us to rise from one step to the next, or in the Bible's words, that take us from glory to glory, from faith to faith, dimension to dimension in God. We get higher, closer and further into God's heartbeat, and begin to manifest that which we are called to do in this life.

So when we look at our lives, we need to realize "what is it I need to think?" and "Why do I need to think that?" because what you think will impregnate you, and you will become that. Understand the concept that naming something creates its nature. Whatever we empower by giving it our attention is "named" and given nature to. Just as giving attention and devotion to an idol causes it to become a "graven image," so will anything we give our attention and devotion to. That's why the Bible says that money is a root of all evil, because when we focus our attention on it, we empower it and make a "god" of it. But if you use money without loving it, that root is cut off. It empowers you to do the things that build your life. God has no problem with you having money, as long as it does not become a god and take his place. When we keep money in our outer court, and use it according to the purposes that build our lives, we can think it and visualize it and have more of it, since thoughts become things, but we need to prioritize it correctly to know how to handle it. It's that same way with relationships and every other thing in our lives. This is the healthy way of using the Law of Attraction.

Think the thoughts of God that need to be in your life. You can't imagine or measure how much God wants to bless you with anything spiritual or natural, but you need to make sure that before you start thinking, you become the observer and controller of your thoughts. You need to strategize and plan what you think, to decide what is beneficial to the real you. When you do that, nothing in life will be hard for you. You will never suffer or be in lack. You will always have an abundance of exactly what you need for your life, exactly what you and only you need to be the overcomer that God has called you to be.

*"We need more than just the Law of Attraction. We need to connect with its more successful twin, the Law of Generosity. And further entwine ourselves with their parent; the Law of Love."*
**Steve Maraboli**

# Putting it into Practice

In this chapter I will present some principles that others have written about which will help you to use the Law of Attraction to your benefit. Different people will use different words and terminologies to describe the same thing because of their different life experiences and this can empower us to see things in a new way. We all need each other, and each person has a unique way of expressing things. When we all come together things begin to happen. In the Book of Acts, when the disciples were gathered together in one accord, the Holy Spirit fell. Things begin to happen - signs and wonders occurred. So when we come together with our different experiences and our different ways of looking at things we can receive fresh insight into things we thought we knew everything there was to know about. Another person's insight and terminologies can bring a new revelation what will penetrate you and set you free in a way that the terminologies you had previously learned couldn't. So it is helpful to know how other people see things.

One Scripture that has influenced much of my thinking is Proverbs 23:7 "As [a man] thinketh in his heart, so is he." The Hebrew word for 'think' in this verse is very interesting, because it is a verbal form of the noun 'gate.' "As a man has 'gated' in his heart." You have to understand that the city gate was the place where judgment is rendered, disputes are settled and deals are made, so it means what you have settled in your heart. Note too that the verb is in the "perfect tense" in the Hebrew. The Hebrew verbal tenses have very little, if anything to do with time. They are concerned with the quality of an action - whether it is complete, whole or finished (perfect tense) or incomplete, incipient or recurring (imperfect tense). So if an action is stated in the "perfect tense" is a 'done deal.' You have settled the matter in your heart, and it doesn't matter whether it happened in the past, the present or will happen in the future, it is a certainty. The essence of your reality, of everything you've ever thought you could be is wrapped up in the thinking of your heart. So it is vitally important to focus on what your heart is really saying. What does it believe? What does it want to say? What does it "know" to be real? Because whatever it "knows" to be real is what you are going to end up having in your life.

## *Clearspace*

The first principle to understand regarding the Law of Attraction is *Clearspace*. We have to clear space in our whole being - spirit, soul and body to make room for the good things God wants to bring into our lives. Clear your spirit through prayer, fasting and meditation. We have to shift from the kingdom of darkness (negativity) into the Kingdom of Light, (the positive). We have to move over into God's kingdom of unspeakable Joy; move over into the unlimited dimension of spirit so that we will have open room for new things to come in.

We have to rid our minds of disbeliefs, fear and anxiety. We have to clear our minds of all the junk that we have learned from our peers, our families, and our teachers. Many of us have been taught that we are horrible, no-good, rotten sinners. God never created anything that was not good. God could never make anything that was half-finished or unproductive. God can only create out of himself, of what he is, which is good, great, wonderful, magnificent, joyful, unlimited; full of Glory. He can only produce that which is inside of him. We have to clear our old ways of thinking about who we are and understand who we are in God. Pray that God will release your mind from all the old junk, and once he has, never turn back. Stay open to signs from God that show you the way to a new assignment that has been formulated just for you.

Some people believe that there is too much emphasis on positive thinking, that some preachers spend too much time talking about the power of positive thinking. What more do you want someone to talk about? The opposite of positive thinking is negative thinking. Should we preach negative thinking? In Isaiah 43:19 we read, "I will even make a way in the wilderness and rivers in the desert." John the Baptist echoed this when he quoted Isaiah, saying he was "the voice of one crying in the wilderness 'prepare the way of the Lord'." God will make the crooked paths straight. Crooked paths represent negativity—fear, unbelief, doubt; things you don't want in your life. Clear out the doubt and fear in your mind until nothing remains but happiness and joy. Change your mind by renewing it in the presence and mind of God and say, "no longer will I think negatively. I won't even dwell on the memories of negative thinking. I'm going to start thinking positively, I'm going to shift from the kingdom of darkness into the Kingdom of Light."

Clear your life of relationships that have brought you bad things that you need to be healed or delivered from. You may need to clear your physical space from the clutter of things you don't need, from things you used in the past, but that don't serve you any longer, or things that simply distract you from the greater purpose in your life. You have to clear all of the junk out of your life in order for the Law of Attraction to work for you in a positive way. Then you open up the airwaves for your Heavenly Father to work for you through the Law of Attraction to bring you the things you desire, that will add to your life.

You have to remember, nothing in the universe can complete you. You are already complete in God. You have to move into the place of already having been made whole, not lacking in anything. God, through the Law of Attraction, can only bring you things that can complement you, not complete you. You must understand the difference. Nothing in life can complete you—not money, not a new job, a new car, a new relationship, a child; none of these things can complete you. You have to know that you are already complete and whole. Everything in your life should complement the wholeness that you already are.

## Clarity

The second principle is you have to get *clear*. When it comes to manifesting your desires you have to have clarity. You must have clear intentions for what you want to call in. Otherwise, you can manifest a lot of things that you don't really want. You have to focus on what you desire and make a list of everything that goes along with it. So if you want a new job, you have to think about everything that is important to you; that makes you happy. Maybe it's the office, the salary, the people you work with. Don't be apologetic about it. Tell the Universe, tell <u>God</u>.

Creation moans and groans, waiting for the manifestation of the Sons of God (Romans 8). It is waiting for us to shift, to awaken, to come forth with clarity and tell God what it is we are looking for. The Scripture tells us that because of the fall of Adam, all of creation fell with him. Adam consciously fell out of the Mind of God into the mind of Adam. He fell from an unlimited state of being where he had the power and potential to Name the animals. Remember, "to name" in the Hebrew and Greek is to give nature or identity to something. So Adam had the power to speak a word into an unformed animal and give it its nature. When Adam said "lion", instantly the power and majesty of the nature of the lion was manifested. The power of the voice, coming from the Mind of God working in Adam, spoke into being the nature of the lion, the tiger, the bear, the butterfly, and the mouse. He gave each of them their nature, their form, the sound of their voice when he named them.

Adam fell out of the Mind of God into the mind of Adam. Out of the Unlimited into the limited. Now we have to get back into the Mind of God to speak into our lives the things we want in an unlimited way. If you speak from a Man's point of view, from fallen, limited mentality, you will produce things that are limited, and really not good enough for you. When you think from the fallen, limited mind of Man, all you will ever focus on are natural, materialistic things, because the flesh and the body always want to pull into itself the things it can relate to. Our body can only relate to new homes, cars, etc. There is nothing wrong with material things. But where we get into trouble is when we don't bring an intention and a definition to these material things. What are we going to do with this car, with this house? Will we use this car to transport someone else who needs a ride? Will we use this house to give hospitality to people who need a place to stay, or maybe to raise a family and teach our children that they are made in the image and likeness of God? How will these things benefit not just us, but others? How will they empower the world? How will they help us bring others to a higher place of consciousness?

We have to clear our space, and then get clarity about what we need. Creation has been brought down to the standards of Man, as opposed to being raised up to the vibration or frequency of God Almighty, the powerful place of glory where creation once was in the unlimited glory of God. Adam was so powerful that when he fell, he caused the whole creation to shift in a downward spiral. Creation suffers like Man suffers. So as we have been awakened back to the Mind of God, Creation wants to be awakened back to its original state of glory, where the lion and the lamb lie down together and the lion doesn't devour the lamb. Where the trees don't die, but grow constantly and give their fruit in every season. Where there is no bad, no hatred, no dysfunction, and no fragmentation. You and I have never seen the power of creation raised up to the limit and the standard it's called to be in. We cannot imagine the beauty contained in nature; that cannot yet be released in this natural, fallen state of being. Because of what Adam did, creation fell and all of its beauty is locked up inside of itself.

Creation, the Universe, is moaning and groaning because it wants to be released, as you were released through Christ, by moving into the Mind of Christ to know that "what I speak I become"," what I think I will manifest." And because of that, Creation relies on you to begin to speak, to re-align yourself. Paul tells us in Romans 8 that the creation waits in eager expectation of the manifestation of the Sons of God. The word *manifestation* in the Greek literally means to "remove a veil". The Bible speaks of us, the Church as the Bride of Christ. Now, before she is married, the bride's face is covered with a veil. Then after the couple has said their vows and the minister pronounces them married he says, "You may kiss your bride." The veil is lifted and they kiss. While the veil is over her face, you cannot see the bride's beauty clearly. Once it is removed, you can see the beautiful, strong, loving, creative, amazing person she is. Has the bride changed any just because the veil was lifted? Of course not. She was that same beautiful, strong, loving, creative, amazing person all the time; you just couldn't see her clearly. John tells us in his first letter, chapter 3:2, "Beloved, *now* we are the children of God, though it can't yet be seen what we are..." (Emphasis mine). We have to shift our thoughts, re-position our understanding of who we are. We have to re-align our thinking so we understand that we are *now* the Bride of Christ, we are *now* the Sons of God. Even though neither we nor others can clearly see who we are, when we look at ourselves in the perfect mirror of the Word of God, we understand who we are and who we have always been in Christ. Beautiful, strong, loving, creative, amazing.

Creation is waiting on you to re-position, re-align yourself to where you need to be so it can be set free. If you're set free, creation begins to be set free. God gave Adam *dominion*, that is, he made Adam lord and king over the garden. He was given the task of tilling the ground all the days of his life. So the earth relies on Man for its release. Creation longs for Man to release it by re-positioning and re-defining, re-titling ourselves back to who we are, back to what we're supposed to be—speaking and thinking exactly like God! Just like Adam did before the fall of Man. So the Universe, Creation, wants to bring things to us that will awaken and re-position us.

Baalam's donkey is a good example from the Scripture. Creation used a donkey to speak to Baalam, because he was blind to the spiritual reality in front of him, and was beating the donkey. Creation, in the form of the donkey, used its mouth to say, "What are you doing? What are you thinking?" to re-position and re-align him. If we are aware, God will use creation and move to us, to put in front of us things that will cause us to think in new ways, to re-position and re-align ourselves.

The word repent means to change or shift our minds, our thinking from a mind-set of negativity to a healthy, positive way of thinking. We have to shift our consciousness, our thought processes, and our minds. When we do this, we automatically begin to shift our lives. Thoughts become things—if you don't like what you're producing in your life, repent, change the way you've been thinking, shift your mind. Alter yourself to "come up higher" like John the Revelator. God told him, "If you want to see things to come, come up higher." Shift your consciousness to a higher place in God so that you are moving and operating in the Mind of God, and all of a sudden you will begin to see that because you have cleared your space, you've gotten clarity, you have thought, felt and believed, a new awakening happens in your consciousness. A new thought begins to come. The positive will automatically replace the negative because you have renewed your mind and positive things begin to replace the negative junk that you have thrown out.

All this goes to say, we have to get back to the way we are supposed to be thinking, and then we will begin to manifest things that we think and be and have in accordance to the way we were created in God before time began. We have to awaken back to the place we're supposed to be. To awaken to the fact that we are a spirit having a human experience. We are unlimited, and we have to awaken that unlimited capability, possibility, and imagination in us. We have unlimited resources of imagination available to us. It's time to wake up that which sleeps and slumbers. Awaken and cause your thought processes to start thinking like God, so you can be free, your family can be free, and Creation is beginning to be free, and delivered from the curse that <u>you</u> put on it when we were in Adam before the fall.

## *Think it, Feel it, Believe it*

So we have *clearspace*, we *get clarity*, and then we have to *think it, feel it and believe it*. Think what you want. When you were growing up your parents told you, "you need to think about what you did." People naturally understand the importance of thinking. When your parents saw you do something stupid like touch a hot stove, your mom said, "What were you thinking? You've got to learn to think!" When you get in a fight with another kid, and come home bloody and beat up, your mom says, "What were you thinking? You should know better." "If you stick your hand in a bee hive you're going to get stung - what were you thinking?" Your parents may not ever have heard of the Law of Attraction, but they automatically knew the importance of thinking that is critical to the operation of this law.

Many people don't know the power of the Law of Attraction, and yet they operate by its principles. Are we putting the power of the Law of Attraction above God? Absolutely not. God works through the Law of Attraction. God is the Author and Initiator of our faith, He is the author and finisher of every principle in the universe, every law that's been given. It's just like the law of gravity. We don't magnify the law of gravity, but I don't care how much you rebuke it, or bind it or pray against it, you are subject to its rule! If you jump off the top of a building, the law of gravity is going to be your god at that moment! You're going to fall and hit the ground. The law of gravity rules over you because you're in its zone, its sphere of influence. If you go to Mars, you will no longer be in the zone of earth's gravity; it won't have any noticeable effect on you, because you are no longer under its sphere of influence (although you will be ruled by the law of gravity on Mars). You are under the rule of the law of gravity, and it will work for you as long as you work with it. It's hard to walk or drive, or even eat a bowl of cereal without gravity, just look at how astronauts in orbit have to deal with such ordinary activities.

These are Kingdom Principles." Seek ye first the kingdom of God and all these things will be added unto you." (Matthew 6:33) Notice that Jesus didn't even say, "seek the King (God)", even though we know that we are to seek after God, the King of the Universe. But he said to seek the kingdom. We are called to seek the fullness of the kingdom. And in that fullness there are kingdom principles such as the Law of Attraction. There are other kingdom principles that govern the universe, such as the law of gravity, and the law of vibrations. The Law of Vibrations states that everything in the universe has a frequency or vibration, and it depends on your attitude, how you're feeling, on your thoughts. If you're down and depressed, you experience a lower frequency of vibration. If you're happy or excited and cheerful, you experience a higher frequency of vibration. You've got to learn how things function behind the scenes.

The worst thing you can ever do is to not understand what happens behind the scene. If you've been given a part in a movie, and you're on the set, if all you're focusing on is the movie, the other actors, then you'll be in trouble. You have to pay attention to the directors and do what they say when they say "cut" or "take 1." If they make changes in the script and you don't pay attention to what they want, you're going to be out. You have disconnected yourself from what's behind the scene, the producer and director. When you actually watch the movie, you never see the producer, the director. But without them, the movie would never get made. You cannot detach yourself from what is behind the scenes. That is what puts you in the movie! You have to obey and abide by the rules of the unseen realm. If you don't pay attention to the director you'll be out of a job and thrown off the set. The same goes for the real world. We can't see the principles of the Law of Attraction, the Law of Gravity, and the Law of Vibrations. We can't see how these principles work because they are behind the scenes. But we know that they are true and accurate because we can observe their effects. We have an eye to see and an ear to hear beyond our flesh, beyond our physical bodies what goes on in the unseen realm of the spirit. We can trust spirit, God, the Mind of God, to lead us, to know how to make these principles work for us and not against us.

We suffer from a lack of knowledge. When we have knowledge and activate it, it is powerful. When we understand the principles, the laws of the unseen realm, then and only then will we be "on top of the game." Then and only then will they work for you and not against you. So is the law of gravity your god? No, but it does rule over you. If you get on top of a building and jump off, you will fall. The law of gravity has a "higher power." God, the Great I AM of the Universe has established the Law of Gravity, and told it what to do, and it has no choice. He gave it its definition, and it cannot bend or break the rules. It does what God told it to do. So if you are depressed, and climb up a tall building to jump off, the law of gravity doesn't look at you and decide that it's not going to work for you, that it will let you jump off and just float. It has no feelings. It has to do what God told it to do, and if you jump, you're going to fall.

The same is true for the Law of Attraction. God established this principle, this law, and gave it its rules that it is bound to obey. Thoughts become things; like attracts like; what a man thinketh in his heart, so is he; what you think about you become. That is how the Law of Attraction works. Whatever you think about and focus on, you get on the same frequency, and the universe says, "It's my job. BAM, there it is! I'll bring to this person what they're asking for."

Like attracts like. We see this all the time. Alcoholic hang out with alcoholics. Drug dealers hang out with drug dealers, Cocaine users with cocaine users; pregnant women hang out with pregnant women. It's a universal principle. Or take religion: church people hang out with church people; Spiritualists with spiritualists; Methodists with Methodists; Satanists hang out with Satanists! It's a universal principle that God has initiated. It does not bend, it's not flexible. It only gives to you what it is programmed to give to you, which is whatever you are thinking. It has no choice no option. If you think murder, it will bring murder. If you think joy and abundance, it will bring joy and abundance. If you think *Agape* Love, it will bring God's *agape* love. God will bring to you the desires of your heart, what you are thinking. So it's vitally important that we understand and use correctly these principles, especially the principle of the Law of Attraction.

You *clear* your space, you get *clarity*, and you *think* it, think it, and think it. Then you have to *feel* it. What is a feeling? The Bible says we don't go by what we feel, and it's true, but feelings have power. If we feel joy, it is because our heart is joyful. If we feel anger, it's because our heart is angry. If my heart does not like you, can't stand you, than I will never be happy to see you. You will never feel peace and joy and pleasure and hug and kiss and love on someone when you hate their guts! Your feelings back up what your heart prophesies. If your heart prophesies joy, you will feel joy. If your heart prophesies defeat, you will feel despair. Your feelings only back up what your heart is prophesying.

Then after you *think it* and *feel it,* you've got to *believe it.* Belief is the strongest thing in the universe! Everybody on planet Earth believes in something. Everybody anywhere in the universe believes in something. Belief is powerful. And everyone tends to communicate with those that share the same beliefs. People fill their lives with people who agree with them, who believe like they do. No one is going to fill their life with people who disagree with them. If you feel you are right with God, but someone else believes that you are in deep, dark sin, you're not going to hang out with them. Your belief is different than theirs. So you are attracted to people who believe like you do. It's automatic. Whatever you believe, you will be attracted to people who believe the same way.

It's actually important to fight against this tendency. You will automatically associate with people who believe like you do, because you feel comfortable and confident around them. But you should try to break this pattern; because it is helpful to have some people who do don't believe exactly like you do. They help you to stay open-minded. They help you to grow and expand. They help you examine your beliefs, and define them and defend them, or even to reexamine what you believe and be open to change. If you are not open to change, then you're stagnant, stale, and dormant and you'll never grow.

When the woman with the issue of blood touched Jesus' garment and was healed, Jesus told her that her faith, her belief was what made her whole. Belief is powerful. In Hebrews 11:1 we read "Now faith is the substance of things hoped for, the evidence of things not seen." Faith is a substance of things that you are hoping for, the evidence of things you cannot even lay eyes on, you've never seen before. Belief is powerful. Your faith, your belief system is what keeps you going. Without a vision the people perish (Proverbs 29:18). If you don't have a vision for something, then you don't have a belief in something. When you have lost all hope, you've lost all vision. You are perishing, the world is closing in on you; you are depressed and suicidal because you cannot see past the present moment.

You don't see any hope in the future even though God promises us hope and a bright future. You will see nothing what-so-ever in your future because your world closes in on you when you feel depressed and down. You have to believe in something. You have to stretch your vision and faith to start believing that all things are possible to those that believe, because they are!

If you believe in God, and believe that your mind is unlimited; if you believe that nothing is impossible for you, and if you believe that "whatever I think I manifest"; and if you believe that "like attracts like", then you're going to have the power of the Law of Attraction work strongly in your life, like you've never known before. Your belief and your faith will activate something in your life to bring to you the desires of your heart.

## *Chill*

So you *think it, feel it* and *believe it.* And then the next thing is just to *chill.* You have to sit back, relax and just chill. If you are anxious, if you are in a hurry to see results, if you get frustrated or confused you will actually impede the action of the Law of Attraction. You can't be impatient. It's not magic. You can't wave a magic wand, say "abracadabra" and get what you want. Your fairy godmother is not going to instantaneously turn a pumpkin and some mice into a carriage pulled by four magnificent horses! The Law of Attraction works through a life-style of a thought process.

Do not be anxious because one negative thought popped into your head. Scientists say we think about sixty to sixty-five thousand thoughts a day! And for most people, eighty to eighty-five percent of those thoughts are negative. That is really sad. But we have the power to re-train our minds. Through the Word of God we can re-train our minds by focusing on the Mind of God. And when we do, we see that his thoughts are nothing but pure, and great, and joyful and positive. We have got to re-align our minds to think like God. We have to shift our minds, so we know what we are going to manifest in our lives. A 'one hit wonder' negative thought is not going to cause your life to spiral down. What is important is what are you consistently thinking of? What are you constantly focusing on? You're human; a negative thought is going to pop into your mind once in a while. We are not yet perfect, we can't avoid that. But we can shift our lifestyle to where the big thoughts will be constantly positive thinking, positive manifestation, positive reality of what we want to manifest in our life, and we'll have that thing. We have to shift our mind and restructure our brain to start thinking of what we desire, what we want to see: joy and love and money and abundance and all the great things that God wants for us and has promised us - but you have to reach up and grab it!

The Scriptures tell us in Proverbs 13:22 "...the wealth of the sinner is laid up for the just." What does that mean for us, "The wealth of the wicked is laid up for the righteous?" It means that it is set aside, but it isn't yet yours. God uses the Law of Attraction to lay up all the good things that he promised you. Even Jesus is held up in the heavens! In Acts 3:21 we read, "[Jesus], whom the heavens must receive until the times of restitution of all things." What if all the promises (and Jesus is promised to you), all the promises that are "yes" and "amen" to you, all the things that God wishes, wants, promised you to have, and died for you to have are held up, are laid up? Because the wealth of the wicked is laid up for the righteous. Everything that you are looking for of wealth-consciousness, of wealth-reality, riches both natural and spiritual are laid up on a shelf! It hasn't been loosed, it's laid up. In order to loose it, you have to manifest it, and you have to create what it is you're looking for. You have to connect with that substance; that promise, that abundance of wealth you know is yours. You have to connect with it. Your thoughts pull it off the shelf and cause it to manifest in your natural reality.

If something is laid up, and you don't focus on it being released to you, the things that you are looking for and need for your life will never come to you. You have to take corresponding action to your faith. You have to do something about it. You have to start thinking it. You can't reach your natural, physical hand up and grab it. The natural cannot connect to the spirit and the spirit cannot connect to the natural. The only conduit between the natural and the spiritual is your mind and thoughts. When you begin to play out the movie of the things you imagine and desire, what you want and what you know God has for you in your heart and mind, something begins to happen. Something begins to manifest. When you play out this amazing movie in your mind, your conscious mind begins to say, "Ah, this is the movie of her life." It doesn't matter to your mind whether you are living it out or just thinking it, it becomes real to you. You give attention and focus to this amazing movie of your life that you have created. You pour the energy of your thoughts into this movie and you give intention to it. You give definition to it, and you empower it. And therefore you create the avenue for the things you need and desire to begin to flow from where they are stored up in the heavens into your life, to manifest in your reality. That is the purpose and the power of your creation manifestation. You have to learn to create it first in spirit. Because the only avenue to connect the spirit to the natural is through your mind. You can't take your natural hand and reach into your heart and pull out something. You can only do it through your thought processes: that is the open door for the things that are stored up for you in the heavens to come through.

So you begin to think it, feel it and believe it, and you create the open door into your world. Your mind and your thoughts are the connection between the spiritual and the natural. That's why Jesus was able to know the thoughts and intentions of the hearts of the people around him, because he was the only one who could shift between the natural and the spiritual. So he knew what these people were thinking, what they were waiting to manifest in the natural. He knew the world that they would create for themselves, what would become of what they were thinking, and could prevent it. That's why Jesus taught in parables—so he could bring us to the place where we understood more about the kingdom. So we could have more revelation about how to make the connection, and how to shift and change our lives. That's why John the Baptist's message was "repent, repent, repent." Because if I change what I am thinking then my thought processes will shift, and my world will not be in a downward spiral. I can shift to a higher consciousness, a higher way of living, connecting with God more intimately, to be able to bring to me what needs to manifest into my life. And from that point on, my life begins to change. That's how the Kingdom of God is. You have to be able to connect to God consciousness in order to manifest in your life what you want. So you have to learn to *chill* on the subject. Once you clear your space, you get clarity, you think it, feel it and believe it, and then you have to learn to chill. The Bible says that the battle is the Lord's. You have to chill, and stand in faith to believe. You don't have to worry or fight for it. All you have to do is bring forth creation manifestation in your thought processes. Think like God thinks and it shall become of you. It will manifest in your life. What you desire, and plan and create in your mind, and the thoughts you are thinking will begin to manifest in your reality. All you have to do is sit back, be still and know that he is God.

When you become still and know that He is God, and chill, you get rid of anxiety. Anxiety will block your blessing, because it comes from fear and doubt and unbelief. If someone is about to go on stage in front of a huge crowd, and they are anxious, if you ask them why, they will tell you, "I'm afraid, I don't want to mess up." Their anxiety stems from their fear. Fear was the root of the anxiety. When the root sprouted, it brought forth anxiety. You have to have confidence and then understand that "It is working. It has worked and it will continue to work." So you can chill about it and not be worried or anxious. It's automatically going to work the way it should work. However it turns out is the way it should turn out.

If you have faith and are believing and are manifesting positive things, then the way it turns out is the way it should turn out. You have left no entrance for the negative to come in. You have moved by faith and thinking positively, and created it in your mind, what else do you think you could manifest? It's going to turn out the way it should turn out.

## The Universe has your back

The next principle is "Know that God has your back." "Know that Creation has your back." Let's go even further - "Know that the Universe has your back!" Remember, the universe is *energy*. The universe has thought processes involved in it. Paul tells us in Romans that Creation, the Universe, is upset with you! Why is Creation mad at you? Because it is in a fallen condition, and moans and groans. It's a fact. God said it in the Bible. God made it clear that Creation has an emotion. This is the reality of the Scriptures. Creation has an emotion attached to it. Its upset, unhappy, miserable, it's diseased (dis-eased). So Creation alive.

Creation groans and travails, waiting for the manifestation of the Sons of God. So you can be certain that Creation has your back. Creation knows you did this to it. You were in Adam when he fell and you caused Creation to fall! So Creation is not happy with you right now. But it also knows that its destiny is linked to yours. Therefore it wants you to be re-positioned, to be realigned so that it can be set free. Creation has your back.

How many times in our lives has God, through Creation, orchestrated things to bring you a revelation of himself? Maybe you were in a grocery store, and you caught sight of an apple and God reminded you that you are the apple of his eye? God used Creation, in the form of an apple to minister to you. God used Creation to move you and the apple to be in the right place at the right time that he wanted to give you that message. The Bible tells us that Nature will prove to you, will reveal to you that there is a God. Can Nature bring you revelation? That's what the Bible says. So you have to understand that God has your back. Creation has your back. The Universe has your back. God is the Lord and King over the Universe, and he uses it to accomplish his purposes.

God uses everything that bows to him to cater to you. We can even go farther than that: God even uses things that are outside of Covenant to speak to you! He uses things that hate him and are in rebellion against him to speak to you and bring you clarity. In the Old Testament God used bad kings to speak good things of where they needed to be to people. He even used a donkey to speak to someone! God spoke through a donkey; he spoke through prophets and kings, and even through bad kings. God speaks through Creation. God speaks through the Universe.

Have you ever looked up at the moon, and had a revelation of God, how he functions in the universe, and how beautiful he has made Creation? God, through Creation made sure that that moon was shining brightly, and you were there to see it and receive the revelation he wanted to give you. Because the more revelation you get, the more awakened you become, the more re-positioned you become. The more re-aligned you become. And the more re-positioning and awakening comes to you, the more it comes to Creation itself.

So it's time for us to understand the principle of the Law of Attraction. It's powerful, potent, strong, and you need to get ahold of it. This is the Kingdom of God spoken to you through the entire universe, to get you aligned to where you need to be. The Law of Attraction is powerful. Like attracts like. It works for the just and the unjust. Understand today what the Law of Attraction wants you to do and to say and to be. If the Law of Attraction had a voice and could say just four words to you, it would say this: "THINK LIKE GOD THINKS."

'When the Christ Conscious mind is lifted up to think like God thinks, you will draw all things unto yourself that you need according to the will and pattern God has set before you to have.'

**Jeremy Lopez**

# What Are You
# Attracting in Christ?

*What are you attracting...*You have magnetism, something inside of you that draws things to you. It draws people, situations, things, whatever you are focusing your attention on. We use the term "Law of Attraction" to describe this phenomenon. Thoughts become things. What you focus your thoughts and attention on is manifested in your life. This is not a process of a single; random thought suddenly coming to pass in your life. If you think of something bad, that doesn't mean it is going to happen. The things we draw to ourselves are those things we continuously focus on. It is a lifestyle of a thought process. What we understand from the scripture "As a man thinketh in his heart, so is he" is that it is a pattern, a habit that you continually, consistently live out. It is what you feed with your attention. I like to use the word *energy*, which comes from the Greek word *energia.*

Our thoughts are energy, and they energize whatever we constantly think about, and bring it into being. There is an energy inside each of us that attracts to us what it is that we live out in our lives.

*In Christ...* The Bible says, "If you are in Christ, there is neither Jew nor Greek, slave nor free, male nor female" (Galatians 3:28, also see Colossians 3:11). Somehow, being a spirit having a human experience gives each of us power - energy, ability, authority. So many people see themselves as merely human, struggling to reach God. They don't have the understanding that they are spirit having a human experience. They are fighting to reach God, trying to figure out what they need, and feeling like they have been left to their own devices. Their spirits are dormant, and they don't understand how to use the power of their own spirit, the true, authentic self that is unlimited, knowledgeable, knowing the end from the beginning. If that description of the self, the spirit sounds rather god-like, it is. Does this mean our spirit is God? Of course not, but we are made in the image and likeness of God, and all spirit *is* one. There is no separation in the spirit realm. The problem is that we allow our conscious mind to over-ride our spirit and become dominant. The Bible tells us to "cast down vain imaginations," to cast down idols. Cast down mind-sets that over-ride your true, authentic self. Any time a mind-set becomes so strong that it over-rides everything about you, down to the core of who you are, your identity - the spirit having a human experience - it is deception; something is going wrong.

Your mind, will and emotions, the "soulish" part of you, was never made to dominate. It was created to complement, to serve and be submissive to your spirit. We are to be led by the Holy Spirit, and the soul must submit to the Spirit of God, and to the human spirit. When you allow your soul to become dominant, you will be deceived; you will focus on material things. Your mind, will and emotions will lead you down the wrong path because the soul was not meant to lead. Your soul was created to follow and submit to the higher call, which is in Christ Jesus, which is spirit.

We must understand the personality, the character and the power of who Christ is, "the One who was, and is, and is to come" (Revelations 1:8). The One who always has been, who *now* is, and is constantly coming (for you linguists, *ho erchomenos,* a present participle in the Greek). He was, he is and he is constantly the I AMness. That's why Jesus said, "I am come that you might have life and that you might have it more abundantly" (John 10:10). Jesus comes in our Now Moment, where there is no distinction in gender, in nationality, in status. And in that Now Moment, the Spirit of Christ within us is drawing to our spirit everything we need in life: The things we need to communicate with each other, the finances we need and want, the career that we are looking for, the desires of our heart. It is the will and the character of God to draw to us everything that has been uniquely fashioned just for us. No one else knows what you need. Others may think they do, but God is so creative that he made each of us uniquely and individually, and he has given us unique and individual needs and desires. When we understand this, we can receive the rewards and benefits that are waiting for us.

We can see in the life of Mary, the mother of Jesus a good example of how attraction works. Mary was faithful to the call, to the voice of God that came to her, and the *Ruah* Wind of God, the Spirit of God breathed over her and she was impregnated with the Christ. Mary was the first and only woman ever to conceive a baby that was not of this natural world, something from on high, from the Holy Spirit. The Unlimited God impregnated a limited woman and brought forth the Unlimited Christ, the unlimited power, force, presence, friend that sticks closer than a brother, friend of sinners, unlimited love, grace, hope, mercy and peace.

Christ, through whom all things were created, was placed deep in Mary's womb. Christ, the most attractive "thing" in the universe, was like a magnet in her belly. We can hardly imagine what that attractiveness, that magnetism, could draw to itself. Jesus said, "If I be lifted up from the earth, [I] will draw all men unto me" (John 12:32). First of all, Christ is verifying his assertion "I AM that I AM." He is not a yesterday God, he is not a tomorrow God. He IS that he is. If he is lifted up, in the Now Moment; if we consciously raise him up in our Now Moment, he will draw *all* to himself. The word in the Greek is *panta*, "all", without limitation or exceptions. This is much bigger and more far-reaching that you might have thought before. Jesus made it very plain; there should be no misunderstanding. The other thing to notice in this verse is the word *draw*. The word *elko*, in the Greek literally means to draw, to drag, to pull or attract. So we can see the power of the magnetism of Christ. If someone will not come willingly, drawn to him, they will eventually be dragged to him, even against their will. We are told in Philippians 2:10 "at the name of Jesus every knee should bow, of things in heaven, and things in earth and things under the earth." So there are no exceptions. Christ is so powerfully attractive, so magnetic that he will draw *all* to himself, and if they will not be drawn, they will be dragged!

As the baby was growing in her, Mary awakened to the realization that she needed to find her cousin Elizabeth; she was attracted to Elizabeth. Now the angel had told Mary that her cousin was pregnant in her old age, but Mary wasn't told to go to her. Something inside her drew her to make the journey. Mary must have known that Elizabeth would understand what was happening to her. There was a conscious attraction where Mary may not have known why she needed to go, but she knew she had to. Many of us have had this experience where we are drawn to certain situations. People will tell you, "I don't even know why I walked into that place, I just know I needed to." There was an attraction, a drawing, even a "wooing". It is the same when you meet a new person that you are attracted to. You are pulled like a magnet to him or her. She is so attractive that you don't want to take your eyes off her. You are drawn to her presence. We use words like "draw" "attract" or "magnetism" often, because we are attracted to things every day.

Jesus talked a lot about the Law of Attraction, even though he didn't use those words. In the New Testament we find him saying, (in our terminology) "Whatever you believe in your heart, believe it really strong, go there with your mind and you will have whatever you think about, whatever you begin to ponder on." Or in the King James Version, "What things soever ye desire, when ye pray, believe that ye receive them, and ye shall have them" (Mark 11:34). That is attraction. In John 16:23-24 Jesus says, "Verily,

verily I say unto you, whatsoever ye shall ask the Father in my name, he will give it you. Hitherto have ye asked nothing in my name: ask, and ye shall receive that your joy may be full." We know that Jesus is the Redeemer, the Sanctifier, the Justifier, and our Mediator. In what way does he mediate? He is the one who attracts people to himself in order to bring them to the Father. We could read the verse like this: "Whatsoever you ask the Father through the Magnet, he will give it to you." Whatever you are seeking from the Father, you have to use the Magnet.

There are many situations in life where you need a mediator. If you are looking for a job, you need to find someone who works there that has some connection to you - either you know them, or you know someone who knows them. That person is the mediator, the one who can bring you and the job together. You attract that job to you through the magnet, the mediator.

There are many other scriptures where Jesus speaks about what we understand as the Law of Attraction: Matthew 7:7 "Ask, and it shall be given you seek, and ye shall find; knock and it shall be opened unto you."

We see this throughout the Bible. Jesus made it very plain. He is the attraction: "I am the way, the truth, and the life: no man cometh unto the Father, but by me" (John 14:6). Why? Because he is the magnet. He will draw you to God and God to you.

So Mary was supernaturally impregnated with the Christ. Somehow she knew she needed to find Elizabeth. She knew that Elizabeth would understand what was happening to her. She was attracted, drawn to Elizabeth. And when she came into Elizabeth's home, the baby in her womb leapt. Elizabeth was experiencing her own supernatural pregnancy. Elizabeth and her husband Zechariah were childless and past the age where they could naturally have a baby. When the angel announced to Zachariah that they were going to have this baby, the angel had to strike him dumb because of the expression of disbelief coming out of Zachariah's mouth. God didn't want him to speak until he could believe! Then after the baby was born, his mouth was released. He was able to speak and say, "His name shall be called John." Zachariah's first words after his speech was restored was to name, to give nature to, the child that was given to them supernaturally.

Even though Elizabeth's pregnancy was different in that the baby was not conceived by the Holy Spirit, but in the usual way, it was still a supernatural pregnancy since she was past childbearing years. And this child, this cousin of Jesus would prepare the way. He would open people's eyes to allow them to see what was coming after him: the Christ. John's message was a shifting of consciousness for people by bringing them to a place of repentance. To repent means to shift one thought to another thought, to a new way of thinking. Most people think of repentance as being about salvation, changing your mind about sin. But it is more than that. Repentance is not for God's sake, it's for you! You have to continuously shed your old ways of thinking and be open to the new. You have to shift and change. That's what the word really means: *meta-noeo:* change your thinking, a shift in consciousness. We should repent every day of our lives. We want to get rid of old habits and shift to a new thought every day; to go from glory to glory, faith to faith.

The spiritual attraction between Mary and Elizabeth caused them to want to be near each other physically, because of their shared experience of supernatural pregnancies. And when they came together, something began to leap at that moment in Elizabeth's womb. The baby in her womb leaped in response to the Magnet in Mary's womb; "Christ in you, the hope of glory." Why is the Magnet in you the "hope of glory?" Because he will attract to you anything *he* and you need in your life. God will give us the desires of our heart. God has placed the desires of your heart there, and they will find the Christ, the Attractor to attract them into your being, your reality. The Christ in you wants to attract into your life anything and everything that is coming from the desires that are buried deep inside of who you are. When you begin to find the desire of your heart, what you are passionate about wants to match up with the frequency wave or desire that God has set in the heavens.

Too many people are trying to get God to move on their behalf. They plead and beg, in blood, sweat and tears, asking God through prayer to do something for them. But that's not Scriptural. God makes it very plain: "You draw near to me, I'll draw near to you." Instead of begging and pleading, we just need to draw near to him. When the prodigal son returned to his father after squandering his riches what happened? He didn't even get the chance to give his prepared speech. His father showered blessings on him, because he had come back, had come near. The Bible says, "Be still and know that I am God" (Psalm 46:10). In the process of stillness you begin to find the knowing of God. Be still and know that I AM. This is the spontaneous Now Moment of understanding the I AMness of God that works in and through us. Be still so that I can attract and know the goodness, the I AMness that works in me and through me.

Another verse that deals with the attraction is Isaiah 40:31 "But they that wait upon the LORD shall renew their strength; they shall mount up with wings as eagles; they shall run, and not be weary; and they shall walk, and not faint." The word "wait" in the Hebrew means to wait, look eagerly for, lie in wait, linger. But the most interesting part is that the original meaning was binding or twisting strands together to make a cord or rope, and it gets the idea of waiting from the tension or stretching of the strands as you twist them together, (*Hebrew and English Lexicon of the Old Testament*, Brown, Driver, Briggs under *qwh*). So those who bind and twist themselves together with the LORD will mount up with wings as eagles. This verifies the scripture in James that says, "Draw near to me and I'll draw near to you." When you bind and twist yourself together with the power source, that power becomes a part of who you are. It begins to awaken your consciousness to understand that the same Spirit, the same power that raised Christ from the dead dwells in you and will quicken your mortal body (Romans 8:11).

When you bind and twist together with God, when you draw near to the power source which is God, that energy, that anointing, that presence, that glory, that essence, the Father, the friend, the Devine Mind, the Mind of Christ, the source of all there is, you are becoming one with it. It is as if you are taking a piece of clay and merging and pressing it into a bigger piece of clay, until you can no longer distinguish two separate pieces, but they are melded into one. So when we draw near to God, we begin to become one with him.

We are knowing him. "Be still and know" That word 'know' is the Hebrew word *yadah*, "to know intimately such as intercourse", as when Adam knew Eve; as in Jeremiah 1:6, "before I formed you in the womb I knew you." There is an intimacy, an impregnation. Before you were formed in your mother's womb God impregnated you with destiny. He impregnated you with life, with an attraction, which are your desires. You awaken to your desires, and all of a sudden you decide to try doing something because you are attracted to it. You may not use the word, but you are drawn to be an architect, or to take up dancing, something in you is pulling and attracting you to do this thing. The desires of your belly are waking up. So through all of this we begin to understand that when we bind and twist ourselves together with God, something begins to happen. There is action, there is energy; there is a combustion or explosion that begins to happen. When you know God and become one with him, then the power is now inside of you, awakening the desires of your heart. Just like Mary and Elizabeth:

the attraction of the Christ in Mary began to attract the supernatural in Elizabeth. Like attracted like. Supernatural attracted supernatural. And when they came together, they were able to compare their like experiences. When the Magnet in you, Christ the hope of glory, begins to become radiant in you, begins to be the focus and existence of your life, then you have the power and the right (*exousia* in Greek) to begin to attract to you what you need in your life.

Draw near to God and he will draw near to you. You have to cause your thoughts to begin to attract to your life whatever it is you need. The desires inside of you that need to be met. Your desires are calling out to you every day saying "I need to be met, to find my match." Christ, the Magnet in you begins to say, "What is it that you want?" You begin to pray, "God, my desires are this and this and this." You begin to ask and it is given. Because you are making an effort. You are taking corresponding action behind your faith, to attract it to your life. Because what you are attracting that is of the will of God is being attracted back to you. It is looking for you and you are looking for it.

We first have to awaken our consciousness to begin living a life-style of already living from that point of view. God calls those things that are not as though they are (Roman 4:17). God knows the power of thought, the power of saying, of turning something around by re-defining its substance, to draw it and acknowledge it into your life. You think about it and ponder it.

That's why Paul tells us to think about that which is true, honest, just, pure, lovely, of good report, virtuous, praiseworthy (Philippians 4:8), because then you begin to draw that goodness into your life. Peter tells us, in his speech to Cornelius's household (Acts 10:38) Jesus "went about doing good, and healing all that were oppressed by the devil." God through Peter tells us that Jesus went about doing good. Many religious people would say that Jesus did godly things, and I'm sure he did, but we're told here that he did good things. Good is good, there is nothing bad or wrong in saying that you are going to attract good things into your life. You don't have to be pharisaical and say that you only want to attract godly things into your life. If you're going to be like Jesus, he went about doing good. You begin to attract good things into your life, and God is good. In order for you to attract the good things in life, the quality things that you know you need to attract, that will empower you in who you already are, you need to understand that you need to draw near to it first. Draw near to God and draw near to whatever it is that you need to have drawn to you, because whatever you are drawn to is also being drawn to you.

There are good things looking for you! If Jesus went about doing good, there is a goodness inside of you called Jesus. There is a goodness inside of you attracting the good things in life to your life. The Bible says the path of the righteous gets brighter and brighter (Proverbs 4:18). Their path gets more illuminated and then illuminated more than the last illumination. There is an attraction that is pulling a greater, broader, more expanded way of living: conscious living, mental living, social, economic, physical life, the life you're intending and want and desire. Jesus said, "I am come that they might have life, and that they have it more abundantly" (John 10:10). There is an attraction of life attracting itself to you, but you must acknowledge it and meet it half way.

You draw near to God and God draws near to you. Remember that God is the author and finisher of your faith. He is the author of creation who created all things, seen and unseen. He knows that the desires of your heart will attract to you what is good, what is godly, what is from his will, what you need that is healthy and unique and fashioned just for you. Your desires will not lead you wrong if you have aligned yourself with what you know God is leading you into. So you have to start attracting good things into your life by taking control of your conscious mind and begin to focus on the good things that you are looking for in your life, the things that you want and need to empower you, or someone else. Maybe that is a new home or a new car. Or it may not be material things, it may be unspeakable joy.

There are things out there that have your name, and your name only on them. It's kind of like Christmas when you were a child. On Christmas morning you and your brothers and sisters would run to the Christmas tree and rifle through the gifts to find those that had your name on them. And some gifts didn't even need to have a nametag. Maybe you found the bicycle that you had been wanting, or that special doll or toy truck that you just had to have. When you see that thing that you had been desiring and had let the universe (in the form of your parents, or 'Santa') know that you wanted, and then it came to you, you recognize immediately that it is yours, it is what you had been desiring. We understand attraction on the natural level instinctively. But we too often don't realize that it works the same way with the supernatural.

On the natural, 'soulish' level, we easily understand that people with similar interests or likes are attracted to each other. Alcoholics hang out with alcoholics, drug dealers hang out with drug dealers. Like attracts like every day. Christians hang out with Christians. Buddhists hang out with Buddhists, Muslims with Muslims. The same holds true with the races. We are trying to be more integrated these days, but still black people are more likely to hang out with blacks, whites with whites. It's just the way things work. We find ourselves being attracted to people we can most relate to.

How do we draw near to the substance, the desire that God has placed in the Universe for us to attract into our lives? We have to live a lifestyle of thought. We bring our lives into a pattern of what it is that we desire and that we know God wants us to have. When we start focusing our power, the energy of our thoughts on that thing, thoughts become things.

Thoughts are energy. This is not magic. These are Biblical, and even scientifically proven facts. The Bible says, "As a man thinketh in his heart..." We don't think with our brains, at this level. Your heart is where your deepest desires are located. It is where the strongest pull that will draw things to you are. The Magnet of Christ in you wants to draw all (things, men, desires, whatever it is you need) to you. If this works in the natural, soulish realm where alcoholics are attracted to alcoholics, then how much more powerfully will this work when you are focusing the energy of your thoughts on the desires of your heart, your spirit? The true Magnet in us begins to draw or drag to us whatever it is we need. When you understand this, it is like you have a bomb inside of you that is ready to go off. The only thing it needs is the igniter that will let it know what it is you want it to explode in. In what area of your life do you want this explosion to take place?

And when the attractor and the thing attracted meet what happens? When Mary and Elizabeth met, something began to leap in Elizabeth's womb, because the attraction was completed. The attractor had come into unity with the attracted. What God has for us in the universe comes together with the attraction that God has placed in our belly. Out of our bellies will flow rivers of living water. So the attraction side of who I am, which is Christ, begins to attract everything I need. Once I put it out there in my thoughts and say, "this is what I want, what I desire, and so Father, I thank you in Jesus' Name. I thank you in the Magnet's name. God you know I've been needing more money, another job, etc.," so through the name of the Magnet you begin to attract it to your life.

The awesome thing about Christ is that he wants you to have the desires of your heart. He has come to give you life. You might be reluctant to call Christ the Magnet, but the Bible says, "Obedience is better than sacrifice." You need to obey God by acknowledging what it is he came to do. Jesus said he had come to give us life, and life more abundantly. You say, "well that's eternal life." But you have to realize that eternity is now. We experience our lives in time, but we, our true selves, our spirit, are living in eternity <u>now</u>. So the life that God wants us to live starts here, in the now. God wants to bless you in the now as well. That is important because it makes a good witness, a good story, and a good testimony. Besides, God simply wants you to be blessed on planet Earth. End of Discussion.

So you have to learn to go through the Magnet. You have to let the Magnet do his job, but you have to do your part as well, by causing your thoughts to become things. You have to start thinking it and seeing it from the understanding that you are already there. You are already living in that reality. It's already yours, but you have to meet it halfway. "Draw near to me and I'll draw near to you." So Mary and Elizabeth came together, and something leaped in her belly. This shows us that when the mission of the attraction is complete, the moment my desire is met, no longer am I living in the "thus saith the Lord", but "it is finished."

When something has been prophesied to you, until it has manifested, you are living in the "thus saith the Lord," the "can't wait" mentality. Once the attraction completes its mission, something begins to leap. Something explodes. The fire breaks out. The river bursts through the dam. The Word of God in you is like fire shooting through your bones. The combustion, the tenacity, the empowerment begins to happen the moment the attracted in the universe meets the attraction inside of you, which is your desire. That's why God gets the glory for it: because the Attractor, Christ the Magnet loves to give you life, because God's goal is to give you life. Then no longer will you say you are living in the "thus saith the Lord" but you can finally say "and it came to pass."

The secret of the power of Jesus, the Magnet in your life is this: every day of your life you are attracted to things and things are being attracted to you. So instead of letting this happen subconsciously, on "autopilot," you have to take control of it. You need to learn to take control of your life and decide what it is that you are going to attract to yourself. You have to ignite the flames and the passion of that Magnet in you called Christ, because that same Spirit that raised him from the dead also dwells in you. There is resurrection power in you to begin to bring anything to life you need, to redefine things you need, attract things you need. Today, make a conscious decision to pay attention to what you are being attracted to and make sure it is what you plan. That it is on the 'table of what you want to eat for your life.'

If you are hungry for lasagna, for instance, you will go out of your way to go to the store and buy the ingredients you need to make lasagna, to meet the desire of your taste buds. Every day there is an attraction that is taking place, in our lives, in our bodies, soul and spirit. And you need to awaken your consciousness, awaken to the reality of thoughts. Your thoughts are powerful. Your brain consumes ten times more energy per unit of mass than any other organ of the body. Some people believe that the human brain operates much like a quantum computer would, if it could be built. It has been calculated that if the brain were a standard super-computer, it would take more time than the age of the universe to perform all the necessary calculations associated with just one perceptual event! You are sending out your thoughts into the Universe whether you are doing it consciously or not. So you need to take control of your thoughts and know what it is that you are attracting to yourself. Know what you are thinking and make sure you have a strategy and a lifestyle whereby you will continue to attract what it is in your life that you are needing, because the Attractor in you, the Christ in you, the Hope of Glory is longing to satisfy your heart and feed your soul, your body, your spirit with the very substance of life. So you can truly say that you have tasted and seen that the Lord is good. You need to start tasting of the desires in your belly to match up with your taste buds in the spirit and know, "This is what I've been looking for." "This is what has been attracted to me by the Christ that lives in me."

*'Ask, and it shall be given. Seek, and you shall find. These are not thing that automatically happen to you as a person. These require action behind what your heart is desiring.'*

**Jeremy Lopez**

# About the Author

Dr. Jeremy Lopez is Founder and President of *Identity Network International* and *Now is Your Moment*. Identity Network is one of the world's largest prophetic resource websites that reaches well over 153,000 people around the globe and distributes ebooks, books, audio downloads, teaching CDs and DVDs. Jeremy has taught and prophesied to thousands of people from all walks of life such as local church congregations, producers, investors, business owners, attorneys, city leaders, musicians, and various ministries around the world concerning areas such as financial breakthroughs, life changing decisions and discovering your career.

Dr. Jeremy Lopez is an international teacher, dream coach and motivational speaker. Dr. Jeremy speaks on new dimensions of revelatory knowledge, universal laws, mysteries, patterns and cycles. He has a love for all people and desires to enrich their lives with love, grace and the mercy of God and to empower them to be successful. Dr. Jeremy believes it is time to awaken the treasure within people to live out the victorious life that was meant for us. His desire is to live a life filled with purpose, potential, and destiny. He teaches with a revelational prophetic teaching gift that brings a freshness of the word of God to people everywhere.

This is accomplished through conferences, meetings and seminars. He serves on many governing boards, speaks to business leaders across the nation and also holds a Doctorate of Divinity. He has coached and prophesied to those such as President Shimon Peres of Israel, Prime Minister Benjamin Netanyahu, Governor Bob Riley of Alabama, millionaires and many others in the political field. He has traveled to many nations including Switzerland, The Netherlands, Jamaica, The Czech Republic, France, Indonesia, Haiti, Hong Kong, Taiwan, UK, Mexico, Canada, Singapore, Bahamas, Costa Rica, Puerto Rico, etc. He has hosted and been a guest on several radio and TV programs from Indonesia to New York.

He is the author of nationally published books and E-books, including his newest book *Abandoned to Divine Destiny: You Were Before Time, The Power of the Eternal Now: Living in the I AM, Releasing the Power of the Prophetic, Awakening to Prosperity, You Were Born to be An Entrepreneur, Divine Direction for Finding Success, Birthing Forth Your Prophetic Word, The Laws of Financial Progression* and many more! He has also recorded over 125 teaching CDs and has many courses and schools such as *School of the Law of Attraction, School of Thought, Visualization and Imagination, School of Seers, Dreamers and Visionaries, School of Financial Perception and Mental Economics, School of the Prophets Course 101 and The School of the Prophetic Advanced Course.* Many leaders around the nation have recognized Jeremy's ministry.

## *Entrepreneur:*

Jeremy Lopez is an entrepreneur, successful dream and life coach, motivational speaker, humanitarian and teacher. His love and passion for discovering and teaching people how to release the mindsets that holds them back from achieving their fullest potential is what drives him and gives his life purpose and meaning. In the last ten years he has grown three successful companies and written fourteen great selling books.

Thousands of ministers, entrepreneurs and individuals worldwide are currently using his life coaching techniques to develop unstoppable confidence and certainty in achieving their vision, business goals and personal best.

Today Jeremy teaches, consults and ministers extensively around the world and sees life changing results including: breaking free of doubts, fear, uncertainty, lack of confidence etc.

As an inspirational and motivational speaker Jeremy focuses on:

> Strategic Investments
> Business Growth Consultant
> Business Strategy
> Business Processes
> Life changing goals
> Many other avenues and points

33558155R00064

Made in the USA
Charleston, SC
18 September 2014